THE ANIMAL LIFE CYCLE

by Maddie Spalding

Published by The Child's World®
1980 Lookout Drive • Mankato, MN 56003-1705
800-599-READ • www.childsworld.com

Photographs ©: Ken Canning/iStockphoto, cover (foreground), 1 (foreground); Shutterstock Images, cover (background), 1 (background), 20 (top), 20 (bottom left), 20 (bottom right); Cheryl E. Davis/Shutterstock Images, 5; Vladimir Wrangel/Shutterstock Images, 6; iStockphoto, 9, 10, 15, 16; Adriana Margarita Larios Arellano/Shutterstock Images, 13; Rich Carey/Shutterstock Images, 19

ISBN 9781503828445
LCCN 2018944815

Printed in the United States of America
PA02396

About the Author

Maddie Spalding is a writer and editor who lives in Minneapolis, Minnesota. She has written more than 20 books for children.

Table of Contents

CHAPTER ONE

A Constant Cycle

Any living thing that can eat, move, and react to the world around it is an animal. There are many kinds of animals. Some animals are vertebrates. They have a backbone, or spine. Vertebrates include birds, fish, amphibians, and reptiles. Birds have feathers, and fish have scales and gills. Reptiles also have scaly skin. Turtles, snakes, and lizards are reptiles. Amphibians are animals that can live on land or in water. Frogs and salamanders are amphibians. Mammals are also vertebrates. A mammal is a type of animal that produces milk for its young. Monkeys are mammals. Humans are mammals, too.

Many birds, such as robins, care for their young.

Some animals do not have a backbone. They are called invertebrates. Insects and some sea animals, such as crabs, are invertebrates. Other invertebrates include worms and mollusks. Mollusks have soft bodies and are sometimes inside a shell. A clam is an example of a mollusk. A squid is an example of a mollusk that does not have a shell.

Each animal goes through a life cycle. A life cycle is a series of changes. These changes follow a pattern. An animal is born or hatches from an egg. It grows older and can then **reproduce**. Then the animal dies. Its **offspring** go through this life cycle, too. This life cycle is constant.

Blackback land crabs are found along coastlines.

CHAPTER TWO

The Cycle Begins

The animal life cycle begins when an animal is either born or hatches from an egg. Most mammals and some reptiles give birth to live offspring. A few insect **species** also give birth to live offspring. Other animals lay eggs. The eggs hatch and an animal comes out.

Many **predators** hunt newborn animals. Newborns are **vulnerable** because they are small. Some animals, such as cats and dogs, are also blind and deaf when they are born.

Newborn kittens don't usually open their eyes until at least one week after they are born.

Animal Offspring

Some animals have many offspring. Insects and fish lay many eggs at once. A female ant can lay millions of eggs in its lifetime. Many fish lay thousands of eggs at a time, while other animals give birth to just one offspring at a time. This is the case with large mammals, such as horses and dolphins.

Many animals take care of their offspring after they are born or hatched. They protect their newborns in different ways. Some insects will try to distract predators away from their young. Other animals give birth in dens. Dens are hollow spaces, such as caves, that animals use for shelter. Animals that use dens include foxes, coyotes, and bears. Other animals build nests. That's where they lay their eggs. The nests are often hidden among tree branches.

Some animals, including ducks, sit on their eggs to keep them warm.

Other animals are on their own. Their parents do not protect them. A female sea turtle lays eggs on shore. She digs holes in sand and lays her eggs in the holes. She covers the eggs with sand to hide them from predators. But then the female turtle returns to the sea. Once the eggs hatch, newborn sea turtles climb out of the nest. They need to make it to the ocean before predators find them. Predators such as birds and crabs hunt baby sea turtles on land. Some fish hunt baby sea turtles in the ocean.

Some animals feed or **nurse** their offspring. Other newborn animals have to survive on their own. Either way, most animals face threats such as predators and harsh environments. If an animal survives these dangers, it can grow into an adult.

Baby sea turtles rush toward the ocean together. This increases their chances of surviving predators.

CHAPTER THREE

Growing and Changing

After an animal is born or hatched, it grows and changes. Many animals become bigger and stronger as they grow. They learn how to catch **prey**. They develop qualities or physical features that help them survive. For example, many birds do not have feathers when they hatch. Their feathers grow in as they get older. Birds wouldn't be able to fly without feathers. They also need feathers to keep them warm.

When animals reach adulthood, they can reproduce. They **mate** with other animals. Eggs or live babies usually grow in the female animal's body. Most mammal babies grow inside a **womb**. Anything that the mother eats or drinks helps her eggs or babies grow. Female animals later lay their eggs or give birth to live offspring.

Many animals have to hunt for food to survive.

Some insect eggs hatch within a few days. Rabbits carry their babies for just one month. Then they give birth. Larger animals usually carry their babies for several months before giving birth. Elephants carry their babies for nearly two years.

The last stage of an animal's life cycle is death. Animals grow old. Their bodies weaken as they age. Their organs begin to fail, and then they die. Or they become vulnerable and are killed by predators. Some animals have short lifespans. Most insects live only for a few weeks. Larger animals live longer. Blue whales can live for 80 to 90 years.

Baby elephants are called calves.

Human actions can disrupt an animal's life cycle. For example, humans may cut down trees for wood. They may clear forests in order to build farms or buildings. Some animals live in trees. They are forced to move to a different environment. This may make it harder for the animal to find food.

Pollution can also disrupt an animal's life cycle. Humans cause pollution when they burn fuels or when they litter. Billions of pounds of plastic are thrown into the oceans each year. This plastic can hurt and kill sea animals.

The animal life cycle is never ending. Animals learn how to survive through the first stages of their lives into adulthood. Then they reproduce. At the end of an animal's lifespan, it dies. But the animal life cycle continues with its offspring.

Sea turtles sometimes mistake plastic for food.

Animal Life Cycles

Frog Life Cycle

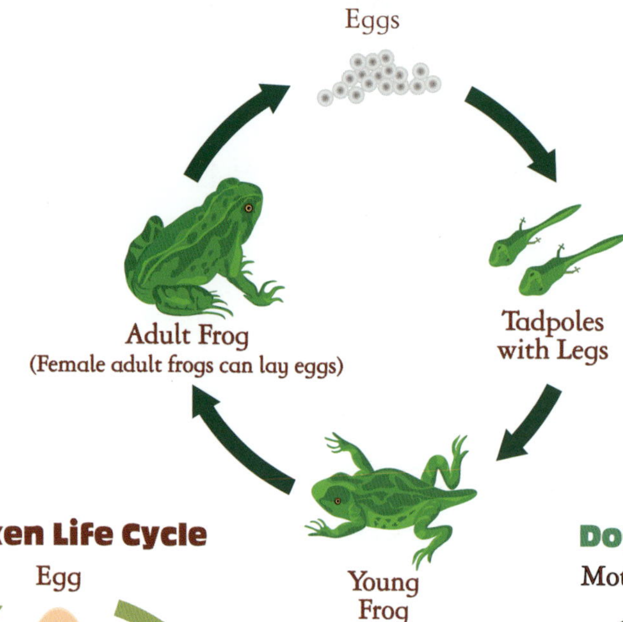

Chicken Life Cycle

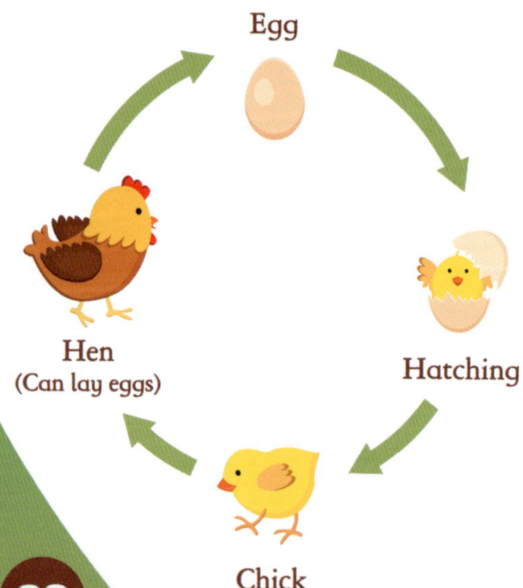

Dog Life Cycle

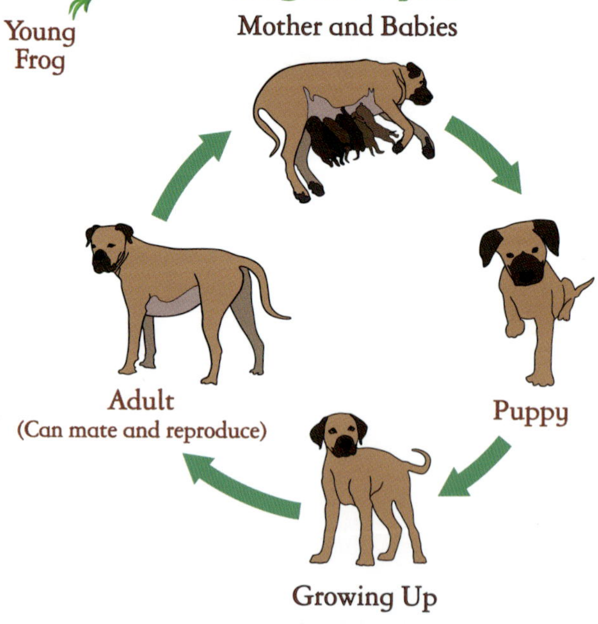

Fast Facts

- Some animals lay eggs. Animals hatch from the eggs. Other animals give birth to live offspring.
- Young animals are vulnerable to predators. Some adult animals protect their offspring by building nests or making cocoons.
- Animals grow from newborns into adulthood. They learn how to survive on their own. Once they reach adulthood, animals mate and reproduce. New animals are born or hatched from eggs.
- Human actions, such as pollution, can disrupt an animal's life cycle.
- The last stage in an animal's life cycle is death. The animal dies, but the life cycle continues with its offspring.

Glossary

mate (MAYT) To mate is to come together in order to make offspring. Monkeys mate as part of their life cycle.

nurse (NURSS) To nurse is to feed a baby mammal milk. Cats nurse their kittens.

offspring (AWF-spring) Offspring are an animal's babies. Animals begin their life cycles as offspring.

predators (PRED-uh-turz) Predators are animals that hunt and eat other animals. Predators need to eat other animals to survive.

prey (PRAY) Prey are animals that are hunted by other animals. Animals hunt and eat prey.

reproduce (ree-pruh-DOOS) To reproduce is to create offspring. Adult animals can reproduce.

species (SPEE-sheez) A species is a group of similar animals. There are many different species of animals.

vulnerable (VUHL-nur-uh-buhl) Something that is vulnerable is helpless to harm or threats. Newborn animals are small and vulnerable.

womb (WOOM) A womb is a place in a female mammal's body where a baby grows before it is born. Most mammal babies grow inside a womb.

To Learn More

IN THE LIBRARY

Dickmann, Nancy. *Life Cycles*. New York, NY: Cavendish Square, 2016.

Marsico, Katie. *Step-by-Step Experiments with Life Cycles*. Mankato, MN: The Child's World, 2012.

Spilsbury, Louise. *Kill or Die: Extreme Life Cycles*. New York, NY: Gareth Stevens Publishing, 2015.

ON THE WEB

Visit our Web site for links about the animal life cycle:

childsworld.com/links

Note to Parents, Teachers, and Librarians: We routinely verify our Web links to make sure they are safe and active sites. So encourage your readers to check them out!

Index